A Man Approved Of God

David J. Keyser, Ph.D.

ISBN: 978-0-6151-6455-7

Table of Contents

I. Introduction

What would you say Christian if I were to tell you that within a short time you could be confident that you were operating in the power of the Holy Spirit most of the time very much like Jesus operated in this power? Impossible? Not according to anything found in scripture. How then? Well, you may have to adjust your thinking, and your beliefs, particularly in one thing; Jesus was like you in his life in the flesh. If you believe that, really understand and believe it, then you will also be able to believe that you are like Him in the power of the Holy Spirit.

It takes a while for this to be established in a person. You do not have to be particularly studious or intelligent to understand. God does not want things to be that way. But you do have to commit yourself to study and be willing to change your beliefs to agree with God as He reveals truth in His written word. Most probably this will challenge your personal "orthodoxy". You may think that I am trying to get you to believe something about Jesus that is not good. You have to be willing to "try it on". If, in the end, you decide that you can not believe this, then you can forget it and throw this little book away. If, however, you decide to press on and are actually convinced that what I am saying is true, then in the end you will have a whole new way of life.

After a while, you will settle down again inside and the short time of relative discomfort will be worth it. No wondering why the New Testament Christians seemed to operate so far above the way believers operate today. No more hopeless feeling of failure in you relationship to God or to His call on your life. Would it be worth it? Are you ready to go on?

Let me assure you that no where in this book am I saying or implying that Jesus was not God or that He ever sinned. Let me say that again. Jesus was God. Jesus is God. Jesus never sinned. When he became flesh, (John 1:14) he volunteered to be subject to the same limits and conditions that you are subject to; the Father and Jesus Himself allowed no way out of this agreement in his mortal life.

When you finish this book - read it as slowly as you want and as many times as you want - you will be assured of Jesus' unity with you in flesh. And you will be assured of your unity with Jesus in the Holy Spirit. This is not a new teaching. It is New Testament teaching which has been lost and hidden from Christians for generations. Now it has returned.

You will know this because you will be established in the truth at the very foundational level. Yes, established, permanently at the deepest level within you. No more wondering when the Holy Spirit might surprise you to bless you or to use you, although He can still do this if He wants. You will know who you are and what you can do from an abiding faith within you. This faith will be based not on feelings, or circumstances, or teeth grinding effort, or mere knowledge, but on a solid understanding of who Jesus was and is and who you are and will be. This knowing is from a firm foundation.

The Gathering Of The People

The largest and most zealous portion of orthodox Christianity today is the Spirit-filled, or Pentecostal, or Charismatic Church. All other groups are either standing still or loosing members as each year passes. There will probably never be what you could call an organizational unity among these churches. If this were even possible, it would most likely be the work of men and women and not of God. There will probably arise new associations of churches which will help mold these churches, fellowships and groups together. But in the final analysis the unity is, after all, a unity of the Spirit in the universal Body of Christ on earth. This used to be called the Catholic Church, in the sense of being world-wide, which should not be confused with the Roman Catholic Church headed by the Pope in Rome. Spiritual unity is really all that is necessary for the Body of Christ to accomplish the task that God expects of it. However, there is so much inconsistency of belief and biblical ignorance in this Spirit-filled church that there is little spiritual unity. Some will say that we need stronger teachings and beliefs in this area or in that. We should know the Bible and we should understand about the gifts of the Holy Spirit and many other things. But our real unity across all denominational lines, denominations old and new, is after all, the unity we have in Jesus Himself. This unity already exists in the Spirit and we are aware of it every time we find fellowship with someone from another group, or church or country who loves Jesus and we encourage one another. But this unity is not strong in what we believe. Granted there are many things about Jesus and God that our minds can not grasp. But God has given us a book called the Bible so that we can understand the things of God which will strengthen us in our faith as individuals and as the Body of Christ. This understanding and unity must be around the person of Jesus Himself. Nothing else will do. Jacob, renamed Israel by God, said "the scepter shall not depart from Judah … until Shiloh come; and unto Him shall the gathering of the people be." (Gen. 49:10) And Jesus Himself said, "and I, if I be lifted up from the earth, will draw all men unto me."(Jn. 12:32) No one and no thing but Jesus can unite the church. He is our standard and our rallying point. His own person is our unity and the Holy Spirit honors any effort that puts Jesus in the center of our understanding and teaching. This is what this book is about, Jesus.

The Offense Of The Incarnation

Long ago in a very important meeting of church leaders it was proclaimed that in Jesus Christ there was a union of two distinct and separate natures united in one Person forever. These two natures are his divine nature, He is God, and his human nature, He is also a man, a human being. A wise man has said that the idea of a God has never offended anyone. All societies recognize some sort of a God, be it a good god or a bad god. What is offensive to the human mind is the idea of a man who claims to be God. [1] Jesus is exactly that. And this Person with two natures is at the same time difficult to understand and the most wonderful thing that there is to know. As Christians we are not excused from considering who He is. In this lies all of our salvation.

If we wish to avoid offense and still retain a belief in God, the easiest thing to do, and this is in fact what has been done widely in the church for centuries, is to affirm His divine nature loudly and forget his human nature. When we do this,

---

[1] Emil Brunner, *The Mediator, A Study of the Central Doctrine of the Christian Faith* (London, Lutterworth Press, 1934), 340.

however, the entire wonderful mystery of "the Word was made flesh and dwelt among us"(Jn. 1: 14) is forgotten.

Believers will easily accept His divinity and even fight vigorously to defend it. But if you try to "flesh out" a true understanding of Christ's humanity, a humanity that was just like our own, the sparks begin to fly. This is because the humanity of Jesus offends people. And it offends precisely because of his divinity. The idea of a man who claims to be God is offensive. He is then no longer remote. He is no longer apart from us. He is no longer far away. He is not avoidable. This offended religious people in Jesus' day. It still offends religious people. They can not keep him at bay. It should not be offensive, however, to anyone who really wants to know Jesus and walk with him as a way of life. To that person his humanity is good news indeed.

It is good news because he has walked in our shoes. He has felt our limitations, lived with them, felt the helplessness, the helplessness that we feel when a beloved relative or friend dies, like Lazarus. If not for the shortest verse in the New Testament, we might be tempted to think that Jesus was clinically detached from Lazarus' death because he intentionally let him die so that he could raise him back to mortal life. But, "Jesus wept." (John 11:35) How many times have we been told that he was weeping because of the unbelief of Mary and Martha and the other Jews. Or that he was weeping because he knew that this miracle would target him for eventual crucifixion by the leaders of the Jews. But what is wrong with the most obvious meaning? Does God indeed give us the scriptures to confuse us? Or are they a revelation? Jesus wept because his good friend went through the pain and suffering of being sick and dying. And Jesus was helpless to stop it because the Holy Spirit hindered him from doing anything. Now, he would raise Lazarus but Lazarus would have to die yet again to wait the final resurrection into a glorious body.

Jesus identified with us so that we could identify with him. So that he could represent us before the Father as a faithful high priest. So that we could have what he has. The man Jesus is an eternal part of the life of Almighty God. And he is our big brother. We are related by blood, natural and redeeming blood.

It is my intention in this book to explain this mystery in a simple and logical way. With the help of the Holy Spirit I will use the right words and you will understand them as they need to be understood. Once you understand with your mind and with your heart, you will never be the same again.

A Certain Mystery

In considering the humanity of Christ while not forgetting His divinity, the mystery of it all should always be appreciated. Even though we strive to understand, there will always be a part of it that we can not grasp. Spiritual things always have a certain mystery about them. This is not a bad mystery, like a crime, but a good mystery that exists because the ways of God are so far above the ways of people. (Is.55.8) If you think that you totally understand, then you do not. After all, "the secret things belong unto the Lord our God; but those things which are revealed belong unto us and to our children forever."(Deut. 29:29) We do not expect to know everything in this life or even in the life to come. We will never be gods. During life in eternity in the resurrection it will seem like we are gods compared to the life we have here, but we do not have the ability to have life in ourselves; we always draw life from God. God has life in himself (Jn. 5:26), that is why he is God.

Things That Do Not Change

"It is common to find Jesus' identity with us in manhood either denied or in various ways curtailed, under the erroneous impression that a deeper reverence is thereby paid to his higher being." [2]

When discussing such wonderful things as we will be considering in this book, it is necessary to put down a few things as absolutes. When talking about such things, sometimes we can become confused and think that someone is teaching something that is bad for believers. Part of this is because of something which has been called "the poverty of language". This means that no matter how many words we use, there never seem to be enough of them or exactly the right words because what we are trying to explain goes so far beyond what we are able to understand. But because we love God and do want to understand the things of God better, we have to use what we have, which is words or language. Also, because the kind of things that we will consider together in this book can sometimes be controversial, it is important to mark out the important things and make them clear. So here are a few things which do not change. Remember that whatever I may seem to be saying in this book, the following are always true. These are not the only things that are true but they are the most important ones. So here goes:

---

[2] Hugh Ross Mackintosh, *The Doctrine of the Person of Jesus Christ* (Edinburgh, T. and T. Clark, 1912), 384.

1. There is only one God.

2. This one God exists as Father, Son and Holy Spirit.

3. This God made the world which can be seen and also all that can not be seen.

4. Jesus Christ is the Son. He is fully God and, since he was conceived in Mary's womb, is fully man as well.

5. Jesus never sinned.

6. Jesus lived the perfect life which was pleasing before the Father and defeated Satan, sin and the world in the flesh.

7. Jesus died on the cross to take away the judgment and guilt of the sins of mankind.

8. Jesus rose bodily from the dead and lives in a place called heaven with God the Father.

9. Jesus and the Father sent the Holy Spirit to live inside Christians.

10. There is one family of God upon the earth and this family can be called the church, the body of Christ, the family of God, or Christians.

11. There are and always have been people on the earth we are not a part of the family of God.

12. To become a part of the family of God a person has to believe in Jesus Christ.

13. When a person does believe in Jesus Christ, his or her sins are forgiven, he or she receives eternal life, and he or she will receive a new resurrected body when Jesus returns bodily and literally to the earth.

14. There is one book called the Bible which has 66 smaller books in it which is the Word of God. This book is the last word on what we believe although often people interpret various parts of it differently.

These truths never change no matter what else happens. They are the most important because all other truths about the Christian faith rotate, as it were, around them. Many Christians who believe differently about other things in the faith still agree on these few beliefs that I have listed here. If at any time you suspect that I do not believe the right things, just refer back to this list to be sure of what I consider to be the most important.

Jesus Was Like You And Me

"If the manhood of Christ is unreal, at any remotest point, God has not quite stooped to unity with man. He has not come so low as we require; there has been reservation and refusal; some part of our burden, after all, has been left untouched." [3]

The one thing that is hardest to hold in our minds is the fact that Jesus was, always was, and is really God, and also that he became a man. He was no less God for becoming a man and he was

_____

[3] Hugh Ross Mackintosh, *The Doctrine of the Person of Jesus Christ*, 404.

no less or more of a man because he was God. When he was on earth for those 33 years, he was both the revelation of God and the concealment of God. He was the revelation of God because He still had the character of God. No one else had that. He was the concealment of God because he left his power behind voluntarily. Because he left his power behind, his glory was concealed. His glory could be seen in his character but not in his power. So his glory was at the same time both revealed and concealed. In other words, people of a childlike faith could see his glory in his character, in his love and understanding and lowliness; "Take my yoke upon you, and learn of me; for I am meek and lowly in heart and you shall find rest unto your souls." (Mt. 11:29) But no one could see his glory in his power because he left it in heaven. Sure, he did miracles among them, or rather, God the Father did as Peter said, but these were done by the Holy Spirit which came upon him as a man at his baptism. We can do similar things by the power of the Holy Spirit just as he did. So you can not say that Jesus was half God and half man because he was all God and all man; only he emptied himself of his power and the glory associated with his power before he came. Only once did the Father allow men to see a glimpse of this power and glory and that was when he was transfigured before Peter and James and John (Mt.17:2). When he was restored to his glory after the ascension, he was restored to all that he had as God before he emptied himself, plus his manhood was also glorified as the "firstborn among many brethren" (Rom. 8:28). Now we can look forward to sharing this glory with him in the resurrection.

Orthodoxy - which has been defined as those beliefs that have been held by most of the church most of the time - holds to both the divinity and humanity of Jesus Christ. However, his humanity has often been neglected. In order for the church to have the vitality and stability that it needs, both the divine nature and the human nature of Jesus have to be understood well by all. It is not my intention here to prove or discuss the divinity of Jesus to any great extent. In the first place, this is a matter of faith and can not be proven to anyone who is determined not to believe it. In the second place belief in His divine nature is much less often unclear in the minds of believers. Suffice it to say that Jesus Christ was and is God Almighty just as surely as His Heavenly Father and the Holy Spirit are also God. Most Christians believe this.

However, when it comes to the true humanity of Jesus, that is often another story. This is not well believed and it is to our detriment. If we do not see the true humanity of Jesus, we do not understand our relationship to Him. As a matter of fact, once we have accepted God as our heavenly Father, as Jesus teaches us to do in the gospels, we have more need of a human Jesus than a divine one. We have a loving Father who is God Almighty and not a man. We need a brother who is not only God but fully human. We can identify with a big brother who knows what it is like to walk in our shoes. The only way to get into trouble here is to say that Jesus sinned because He did not. In every other way He was as human as we are. His mother Mary was no different than any other wholesome teen-age virgin. Jesus gets his humanity honestly from her. But this does not fully cover the subject. If we are to understand just how human Jesus was, (I say "was" for now. We shall look at the "is" later on.) a better and bigger explanation is necessary.

It says in Philippians chapter two, verse seven in the New American Standard Version that Jesus "emptied himself" when he became a human being. He grew for nine months in Mary's womb and was born into our world. An understanding of this "emptying" is the only sensible way to understand how Jesus was truly a man with the limitations of a man while He lived and ministered for over 33 years among us. Once we understand this, the actions of Jesus in the gospels will make sense to us more than they ever have before. We will then be able to see Him as a man of faith operating by the power of the Holy Spirit just as He expects us to do. We will no longer say when we sense that a certain thing is expected of us,

"Well, that was Jesus!" But before launching into this you need to be ready to be stretched a little. You need to be willing to re-think some things that you may have always believed. It may seem threatening or even disrespectful at first until you begin to understand and "balance up" again.

David J. Keyser

II. What Jesus Left Behind

Most every Christian knows that the Son of God changed a lot when he came to earth. We know that "the Word was made flesh and dwelled among us". (Jn 1:14) What is not often clear is everything that was involved in this change. In order to come and be one of us Jesus had to leave much behind. In this chapter we will consider what he gave up to become one of us. This was not some kind of an act that he put on while he was with us. He actually changed to become one of us. When we begin to understand how much he left behind in heaven with the Father, we become even more overcome with the greatness of his love and of the Father's love for us and we begin to realize our own possibilities as believers.

The Three Omnies

In order to become one of us Jesus gave up three of the most important characteristics of God. I call these The Three Omnies; Omni-presence, Omni-potence, and Omni-science. When these words are divided in this way, it is easier to understand them. The prefix "Omni" simply means "All" or "Completely". God is All-present, or everywhere at the same time. In order for Jesus to become one of us he had to give this up for 33 years to live in time and space with human beings.

This is obvious because he took a localized body like every human being has. He could only be in the place where that body was located. He got this body from his mother Mary. It was a body like her body, a human body. When Jesus gave up one Omni, he also had to give up the other two. Omnipotence means to be all powerful. Jesus gave up his all powerful ability to become a man. His heavenly Father retained his power and the Holy Spirit kept his also, but Jesus gave his up for those 33 years. Omni-science means to know all things. Jesus also gave this up to become a man and the gospels are full of examples of things that he did not know. For instance, the time of his return (Matt. 24:36), who touched him when he was in the crowd (Luke 8:45), and the location of Lazarus' body (John 11:34).

Some may ask, "How is this possible? What you are and what you have are yours, unless you become disabled in some way." Jesus did not become disabled in the sense of getting sick or old or infirm. God the Son in agreement with the Father and the Holy Spirit has the ability to give up anything he wants by a simple act of his will. This is not a pretend giving up but a real parting with these abilities. Exactly because he is God, he can do things that we can not do. Why did he do this? His reason for doing this, giving all this up for a time, is his great love for his people. It is not because he failed or became weak but because he loves us so much. "But," someone might also ask, "what about the things Jesus did and knew that were supernatural? After all, he was able to do and to know things that must have needed the very powers that you are saying that he left behind in order to become a man." Those things which Jesus did which were obviously supernatural, he did by the power of the Holy Spirit. These days we call such things the gifts and ministries of the Holy Spirit which are given to the body of Christ on earth, the believers. Jesus did these wonderful things as a man by the power of the Holy Spirit just as he expects us to do them today.

God's Will Is The Most Powerful Part Of His Nature

Christians are often fond of the verse that says, "Your sins I will remember no more." (Heb. 8, Jer. 31) This is good for the believer because he knows that he is completely free from condemnation or personal judgment before God. But how does God do this? The only way humans can forget is when their brain powers deteriorate. But God can decide to forget. His will is stronger than his memory. So when we are brought into the New Covenant, he decides to forget our sins and iniquities. That in itself is a wonderful subject to consider.

Not only is God's memory subject to his will but Jesus' very power as the eternal pre-existent Son is also subject to his will. So is his consciousness of his state in glory. So when he and the Father made their private agreement about what he would do, he decided to put aside his power and his conscious awareness of his glorious state to become a man. When he was born of Mary, only his spirit knew. Here is where it is important to understand the difference between the spirit and the soul or mind. As he grew, he became more and more consciously aware of what he had been. By twelve years of age he knew whose son he was. After he received the Holy Spirit without measure, his human spirit knew all that the Father wanted him to know.

His Glory

Jesus left the three Omnies behind for 33 years. He had them again after his death on the cross and the resurrection. We will get to that also. Another important thing that Jesus left behind in order to become a man was his glory. One way we know this is because he talked to the Father about when he would get his glory back (Jn.17:5). Another obvious way that we know he left his glory behind is in the gospel record. Jesus appeared very much like other men. When the soldiers went to arrest him, they waited for Judas to identify him (Mt.26:48). There was no halo around his head like we see in the old paintings. At the transfiguration (Mt. 17) his glory was seen by a special act of the Father and the Holy Spirit by the three: Peter, James and John. But this was a one time happening. Jesus left his glory behind to become a man. This, like the three Omnies, was not a hiding or a veiling but an actual leaving behind. Consider, if Jesus had not left his glory behind, it would not have been possible for people to even look at him for the brightness of his glory. All would have know immediately that he was God. Faith would not have been necessary. It would have been like the children of Israel in the wilderness when they asked not to be exposed to God but rather that Moses should speak to God for them (Heb.12:19-20). Jesus left his glory behind to become a man.

There was the covenant between the Father and the Son [4]

Before Jesus came, he and the Father made a covenant between themselves. This has been called the Covenant of Redemption. What has been called the Covenant of Salvation is the one that God makes with us as believers. A covenant is

---

[4] Edward Irving, *The Doctrine of the Incarnation Opened*, From The Collected Writings of Edward Irving in five volumes, edited by Rev. G. Carlyle, Vol. 5 (London: Alexander Strahan, 1865), 122.

an agreement between two persons which promises to be concerned foremost for the needs of a person or persons other than yourself. It is based on trust. A contract, which is usually a legal agreement, is not based on trust. God always keeps his covenants even if we do not. God considers a covenant breaker to be the worst sort of person. When it says in I John 1:9 that God is 'faithful and just to forgive us our sins and to cleanse us from all unrighteousness," it is referring to the Covenant of Redemption between the Father and the Son. This covenant can not be broken because both persons involved are God and they never fail to keep a covenant. The Father always forgives and cleanses us because of this covenant and what the Son did to establish it. He established it with his own blood. In this covenant Jesus agreed to live a perfect life for you. He did this and defeated sin in the flesh. He had to deal with temptation and weakness just like we do because his human nature, or flesh, and his body was the same as ours. The Holy Spirit gave him the power to do this. The Holy Spirit gives us the very same power. Our victory is based on Jesus' victory.

The Flesh Of Jesus Was Mortal And Corruptible [5]

The flesh that Jesus got from Mary was mortal; it would die eventually. And it was corruptible; it would decompose in the grave if something was not done to change this. This is the part which is shocking to many people. No, Jesus was pure, Jesus was holy, so he could not have been like us, or even like his own mother. There is no contradiction here. We are not saying that Jesus sinned, or that Jesus was not holy. But we are saying that his human nature, his physical body and his inner human nature, was the same as his mother's. Only the Roman Catholics wrongly believe that her flesh was not sinful like ours. She was like every person descended from Adam and Eve. Jesus' flesh, outer and inner, was like hers; it was hers. Jesus could die physically and he did. If he had not gone to the cross, he would still have had mortal flesh. The Father promised him that he would not see corruption or decay after death (Ac.13:35). This promise would not have been necessary if decay was not possible. Jesus was temptable. If he was not temptable, then the temptations (Luke 4) were yet another show put on

---

[5] Edward Irving, *The Orthodox and Catholic Doctrine Of Our Lord's Human Nature* (London: Printed by Ellerton and Henderson For Baldwin and Cradock, 1830), 108-116.
Edward Irving, *The Doctrine of the Incarnation Opened*, 135.

for our benefit. But it is not a sin to be tempted. It is a sin to give in to it. Jesus did not give in.

But that does not mean that it was easy. He had a job to do which was to defeat sin in the flesh. He had to win where Adam and Eve lost. He had to win where we lose. If he did not win, then all was lost. No one could win. And the battle had to be real, not make believe. (Ro. 8:3) When he won, he won for you. He won for you in two ways. He won for you so that he could go to the cross for you and be the perfect sacrifice. So then by your taking his sacrifice by faith, God no longer sees your sins - ever! But also by winning for you he defeated the flesh in his own life and he can enable you to do the same. Your flesh never improves. It never gets better. Don't let anyone tell you that you can be changed or "sanctified" in your flesh in this life so that it no longer wants to sin, no longer wants to descend into bad things. If you believe that, you will lose a lot and you will be discouraged all your life in your Christian walk. Flesh has to be conquered. It has to be crucified. But Jesus makes that possible for you. You just identify with Jesus. His cross will work for you. You do not have to try to crucify yourself. That will not work.

So now you may say, "I have sent my flesh to the cross for today - we do live one day at a time - now I am going to be holy; but it seems like my life is empty. I am ashamed that I am not content with the Holy Spirit in my life. There seems to be something missing. How can I live? How can I love? How can I relate to people around me? They might pull me away from God. They might cause me to stumble. People are even beginning to say that I act like I am too good for them. What is going on? What has happened to me?" If you have ever had these feelings, you are normal. If you are a sincere Christian, you probably will have these feelings. You are designed to live as a person, as a human being. Human beings have flesh - bodies, minds, feelings. You are not designed to live without them. What you need is flesh that has been fixed, made subject to the will of the Spirit and to the will of the new person that you are in Christ. You want to live to please God. When you are pleasing God, you are pleasing yourself. You want to be free to be human. Jesus has done what was needed for you to be free like this. He will give you his flesh. It has been fixed. That is what the next chapter is about. Get a hold on it and you will never be the same.

Christ Is Fallen Manhood Redeemed [6]

You see, Jesus had to be fallen manhood redeemed. If he had another flesh, then he redeemed another race. But we believe that he redeemed our race, the human race. So his flesh,

---

[6] Edward Irving, *The Doctrine of the Incarnation Opened*, 125-27.

both the outward body and the inward soul, had to be like ours; not just similar to ours but exactly like ours. Jesus had no original sin at any time but he did have the ability to sin. When Jesus was tempted, he could have chosen to give in. Sometimes he even wanted to give in. But he did not. He did not because the Holy Spirit helped him just like he helps us. He did not because he had perfect faith because of the encouragement of his Divine nature. He did not because he stayed in close fellowship with the Father; he prayed a lot. Now we do not have perfect faith, but our faith is growing and Jesus is always willing to let us use his. ("I live by the faith of the Son of God who loved me and gave himself for me." Gal.2:20) We have grace to recover us when we fail. We will consider this more later. And we can spend time with the Father also, although we often do not take full advantage of this privilege. We have to be constantly reminded, and I say it more than once in this book, that temptation is not sin. It is the giving in to temptation that is sin. Jesus was often and sorely tempted; but he did not sin. He suffered more in his temptation than we do because he never gave in. He had to resist it constantly and in doing so he changed his flesh even before the resurrection. He defeated sin in the flesh.

What Was God's Motive?

The reason that the Son came in this manner was purely for love. It was not out of weakness. It was not for any other reason than the love of God for people. It is most important to remember that love alone is the reason that he gave up so much for us. It will help you to remember and to understand that Jesus is both truly God and truly a genuine man. It will also help you to keep from going too far in the wrong direction. Not only did Jesus give up much in heaven when he became flesh, he also gave up many things that we can have as humans in this life. He gave up a permanent home (Mt.8:20). Some will want to say that Jesus was married or sexually active. When Jesus said that some keep themselves from sex for the sake of the Kingdom of God, he was speaking of himself (Mt.19:12). He gave up many human things during those 33 years for the sake of his people.

David J. Keyser

III. Some Important Questions

Now let's look at some examples from the gospels of how Jesus operated as a man.

Did baby Jesus know that he was God?

Did he cry?

How much did Jesus learn about his calling by the time he was twelve years old?

Did Jesus eat a lot as a teenager?

Did he notice girls?

What did Jesus have to learn as he grew up?

What was it like for Jesus when he was baptized and the Holy Spirit came upon him?

Was Jesus caught off guard when he fell asleep in the back of the boat and the storm came upon them? How did he rebuke the storm?

Why didn't Jesus know the day or the hour of his own second coming?

Was Jesus really surprised at the faith of the Roman centurion?

Why did Jesus ask, "Who touched me?" (Lk. 8:45)

Did Jesus expect to find fruit on that fig tree or did he curse it just to teach the disciples a lesson?

Why did Jesus have to ask where Lazarus was buried?

Did Jesus want to get out of going to the cross when he asked the Father to let 'this cup pass from me"?

Was Jesus a better, or a stronger, or a smarter man at age 33 than at 18?

Why did Jesus say that Christians would do the same things that he did and even greater things?

Was Jesus' position in heaven better after his resurrection than it had been before he came to earth?

Some Answers

"In any case, it is only by degrees that the full meaning of his relationship to the Father . . . can have broken on Jesus' mind. The self-sacrifice in which his earthly life originated drew a veil over these ultimate realities. . . we are lead to believe that the veil must gradually have worn thinner and more translucent, until . . . he knew himself the Son conditioned in and by humanity."[7]

What do the answers to all these questions mean to you and to your walk as a Christian believer? Whether or not your life was greatly changed when you became a believer, it will be after you understand the answers to questions like

---

[7] Hugh Ross Mackintosh, *The Doctrine of the Person of Jesus Christ,* 391 and 481.

these? After we have discussed them all, you can then draw your own conclusions.

No, baby Jesus did not know in his mind that he was God anymore than another infant knows his last name or what his father's occupation is.

Yes, baby Jesus cried. Since infants make their needs known by crying, and Mary and Joseph were not perfect parents, baby Jesus would have had to cry to get their attention. Just because "Away In A Manger" says that he did not cry does not make it so. The Bible never says that he never cried.

By the age of twelve years Jesus was beginning to understand who he was and why he was here. This is the age when most people begin to think about "what they will be when they grow up." Jesus was becoming aware of the Father's will for his earthly life.

Teenagers eat a lot. We have no reason to believe that Jesus was any different. Teenagers eat a lot because they are hungry. They are hungry because of the amount of energy they consume to grow and live their very active life. We have no reason to believe that Jesus was any different.

Most all teenage boys notice girls. It is possible for them to notice girls without sinning. Insofar as it is possible to notice girls without sinning, Jesus noticed.

Jesus had to learn what all the other children in Nazareth had to learn while growing up. He helped around the house and learned the carpenter's trade from Joseph. He probably even had to take out the garbage.

It was a wonderful day for Jesus when the Holy Spirit came upon him. He had similar feelings about receiving the power of the Holy Spirit to those of other people. It was also a very serious time because it was the beginning of his public ministry.

Jesus was truly asleep in the boat when the storm came up. He awoke to the wind and the waves and the panic of the disciples. He was not upset and he rebuked the storm. Jesus rebuked the storm by faith, not because he was God. This is an important point because it determines what you will believe about your faith and actions.

Jesus did not know the exact time of his return because the Father by the Holy Spirit had not yet told him.

Yes, Jesus was pleasantly surprised at the faith of the Roman centurion. He was surprised because the centurion was a gentile and a soldier. He was not a Jew. But Jesus was happy to see this faith and held the centurion up as an example to the Jews. Perhaps this even made Jesus realize more fully that gentiles would become promising believers.

Jesus had to ask, "Who touched me?"(Lk 8:45) because he didn't know who it was that touched him. He felt healing power leave his body, but did not know where it went. The Holy Spirit, who was Jesus' anointing, saw the woman and power was released. But the Holy Spirit did not tell Jesus who it was that drew the power.

Jesus expected to find fruit on the fig tree. He was disappointed and angry so he cursed the tree and it died. This was true human emotional involvement. Jesus was looking for another kind of fruitfulness among the Jews and he did not find it. He had a taste for a juicy fig and did not find it. The fig tree took the brunt of his wrath. Have you ever broken a pencil because you were angry at the way someone had treated you?

Jesus had to ask where Lazarus was buried because he did not know where the grave was. Even though he knew that the entire situation was to be to the glory of God and he came to raise Lazarus from the dead, the Holy Spirit had not told him where the grave was. So just like any man, he had to ask.

Yes, Jesus was really asking the Father if the cross had to happen. The pain and the darkness of the cross was horrifying to Jesus and that was why he asked the Father if it had to happen.

Jesus was more mature with all the attributes that come with maturity at 33 than he was at 18 because he grew and changed just like any other human being both in his personal life and in his calling.

Jesus said that Christians would do the same things that he did and greater things because he came as a man to show us the way, and there are more of us than there was of him.

Jesus' position in heaven after the resurrection is even greater than it was before he came to earth. Because after the resurrection Jesus' manhood is fully developed and, what is more important, also glorified. He has a glorified manhood. This humanity is eternal. Jesus is eternally human and has a resurrected body of "flesh and bone" (Lk. 24:39) just as we will have. It is possible for us to have this resurrected body because Jesus has one himself. Before Jesus came to earth in the incarnation, he was God and full of glory as God in heaven, but he was not yet a man. So now he is glorified both as God and as man in eternity. This is a great difference. And it is never ending.

Here is a question that we have not considered so far. Why did Jesus treat the Syro-phoenician woman like he did? Why did he reward her perseverance? "Even the dogs eat the crumbs."(Mt. 15:27) Like everything else that Jesus did, this was not an act put on for our benefit. Jesus believed that the gospel was sent for the lost sheep of the house of Israel. This woman was not of the house of Israel. She was a half breed, part Phoenician which was of Greek extraction and part Syrian which was one of the ancient enemies of the Jews. When she displayed a truly humble attitude, it touched his heart and he was moved to help her. This is the act of a true and loving human being. [8]

---

[8] Alfred E. Garvie, *Studies in the Inner Life of Jesus* (London, Hodder and Stoughton, 1898), 273-4.

David J. Keyser

IV. A Man Approved of God

Ye men of Israel, hear these words; Jesus of Nazareth, a man approved of God among you by miracles and wonders and signs, which God did by him in the midst of you, as ye yourselves also know: (Acts 2.22 AV)

Here Peter makes it absolutely clear on the day of Pentecost that Jesus was a man. Furthermore, he says that Jesus was a man approved of God. Then he goes on to say that the miracles and wonders and signs that were worked were done by God. The primitive church started with the man and went on to recognize that Jesus was also God. This was natural to them. They would not have thought of approaching it any other way. After all, Jesus came to them as a man, they lived with him and touched him and knew who he was. It was only centuries later when the councils of bishops were meeting to combat various heresies that they started with God and also gave assent to his humanity. This stress on his humanity is what gave the early disciples the zeal and confidence they needed to "turn the world upside down."(Acts 17:6) They were of the same humanity as Jesus. He did what he did by the Holy Spirit. So they believed that they, as possessors of this Spirit, could do the same things and even greater things. By the time the church councils were meeting and starting with Jesus the God and admitting to Jesus the man, the power was gone from the church. In their efforts to put down the heresies which denied that Jesus was God, they forgot about his humanity. It was a long hard battle that they had to win and they won it only to find that they had gone off the road on the other side. The Reformation addressed the problem but not fully enough. In the eighteen hundreds the Scottish minister Edward Irving stressed it and a true Pentecostal revival broke out. But the Church of Scotland put him out. Later some other theologians tried to restore the truth of the humanity of Jesus to the church but they were considered to be liberals to Bible believing folk and the word never got out to the membership. Now is the time for all to understand. Jesus was a man. He was a man approved of God which God the Father used to work miracles and signs and wonders among the Jews. He was dependent on his Father to do this through the power of the Holy Spirit because he had left his own divine prerogatives behind for a while.

Basically there are three possibilities

In considering all this basically there are three possibilities. Sometimes it helps to think about the possible alternatives. Either Jesus had two minds or consciousness' in one body, or he was God in disguise, or he emptied himself of his divine powers before he came. Let's consider each of these possibilities. [9]

The First Possibility: God the Son, the second person of the Trinity, came to our world to inhabit a human body. In doing this he was actually two persons in one body, God and a man. He had two consciousness', two intellects and two wills in one body. He was continually torn between acting as the Almighty and acting as a man. His divine self and his human self lived together inside of him and if there was a conflict, the divine side which was stronger would win.

The Second Possibility: God came to earth in a human body disguised as a man. So it was really simply God in a human body. He would purposely act human in the appropriate manner at every stage of his human life. When his body was an infant, he acted like an infant. When his body was twelve years old, he acted as if he were twelve years old. Even when he became grown he would act like he did not know things so that he would fit in better. Essentially, he was putting on a act for our benefit and having the experience of living in a human body. Strangely enough this belief is the one that has dominated the church for centuries.

The Third Possibility: He emptied himself. This is true humanity. He is no less God for doing

---

[9] A.B. Bruce, *The Humiliation of Christ in its Physical, Ethical, and Official Aspects*, Fourth Edition (Edinburgh: T. and T. Clark, 1895), 138

it. As a matter of fact, he is proven to be even more loving and merciful because he voluntarily laid aside his Godly powers in order to become one of us. His character is still the character of God. He is love and goodness and without sin. But he is subject to our weaknesses and has to rely on the power of the Holy Spirit to perform supernatural acts. He exercises faith in order to do these things. The Son agreed with the Father to become a man and to submit to the limitations of a man. He did not change his character. He was still goodness, holiness and truth. But he did give up his powers; he did not know everything, he did not have all power and he could only be in one place at one time in his human body. Since Jesus in this self-limited state was completely dependent on the Holy Spirit to have supernatural knowledge and power, he functioned as he expects us to function. In things not told to Jesus by the Holy Spirit he had to learn and grow just as we do. He matured as a person. Also, due to the agreement that he had with the Father before coming in the flesh, he could not change the rules once his human life started. He was locked in until after he died when he got it all back and more. Yes, more, because he has special honor as a man which he did not have as God before he came. Resurrected he is Lord both as God and as a man. This third view is definitely the best one. Not only because it sees

God as more honest, but it enables Jesus to truly understand us and to show us how to function.

So now that we have an idea of what Jesus left behind lets look at what he brought with him.

Jesus Brought His Personality With Him

Even though Jesus left much behind to come and live among us, he did bring something with him. We do not loose sight of the fact that although he chose to leave the three Omnies and his glory behind, he still had a divine nature while he was here. Some teachers believe in two kinds of characteristics concerning God: those which he can leave behind if he wills to and those which he can not because they are part of his personality as opposed to being part of his powers. Jesus in his divine nature had to bring those things that make up the personality of the divine nature. We can state these things as life, truth, holiness and goodness.

If we think of these things like we do the fruits of the Spirit and if we think of the powers like we do the gifts of the Spirit, perhaps it will help us to understand better. The fruits of the Spirit (Ga.5:22-23) have been called the personality of Jesus and the gifts of the Spirit (I Cor. 12) have been called the abilities of Jesus. If you ask a Christian to choose between the fruits of the Spirit and the gifts of the Spirit, he will choose the fruits. The fruits are better because Jesus said that we would be known by our fruits: love, joy, peace, faith, gentleness, goodness, patience, teachableness, and self-control. And fruit is something that grows in us and requires our cooperation to produce them even though we must depend on the Holy Spirit to provide the seed and the nourishment and the light to grow them. We also have to be "pruned" by the Father and that is a painful process, letting all the weaker branches be removed. The fruits of the Spirit are actually just as supernatural as the gifts. If you try to fake the fruits, they will be exposed sooner or later as false fruits. It is wonderful that we do not have to chose between the fruits and the gifts as they are both available to believers today.

Jesus brought his godly characteristics with him - life, truth, holiness and goodness - from which all the fruits of the Spirit are taken. Jesus said that the Father had given the Son the ability to have life in himself. (Jn. 5:26) This means that the Son also was God. Only God has the power to have life in himself. All other beings who are called creatures draw their life from God both in earth and in heaven. This Jesus could not leave behind. Jesus said that he is the Truth. This is part of his being God. All others may have parts of the truth, but only God is the Truth. We can get holiness from God, but he is in himself Holiness. The same with goodness. Jesus said, "Why do you call me good? Only God is good." (Mt. 19:17) He did not say this because he also had a human nature. He still has a human nature, only now it is glorified. He said this because some Jews were willing to call him good but were not willing to call him God. He wanted them to make up their minds. Jesus could say in all honesty, even though he left some things behind when he "emptied himself" to become a man, "he who has seen me has seen the Father."

What Do We See?

When Jesus said, "He who has seen me has seen the Father," (Jn.14:9) what did he mean? In another place it says, "No man hath seen God at any time; the only begotten Son, which is in the bosom of the Father, he hath declared him." (Jn 1:18). If a person were to look right at God in all his power and glory, he could not stand it. God would not allow His "friend" Moses to see His face. And yet Jesus, who appeared to be just like other men said, "He who has seen me has seen the Father." What was there about Jesus while he was here which could enable him to say that to see him was to see the Father? It was his personality, his character, his goodness and love and truth. This is the essence of God. His glory and his power are things that he carries with him. He can lay these things aside if he wants to. He even laid them aside at certain times in the Old Testament and appeared as "the Angel of the LORD" on several occasions; for instance, to Abraham and to Joshua. But there is still more meaning in these words.

We are made in the image of God. (Gen. 1:27) Now this image is not in hands or feet or ears or any other physical characteristic. The image of God is inside in our ability to think and to speak and to love. But this image has become marred; it has been changed by sin and the results of sin. Jesus was, and is, the "express image of his person," the person of the Father. (Heb.1:3) There are two reasons that he is this "express image" or exact image. One is because when he became flesh, his personality did not change. He was still God the Son. His flesh was real, external and internal, but his person did not change. He actually "became flesh"; he did not take it on as a disguise or some clothing. But his person was the same. Two, Jesus as a man was also made in the image of God. Only for him the image was not marred. In him the image was without sin. He was still vulnerable to sin, but there was no original sin, no bondage of sin. In such a person and in such a man the image of God can be clearly seen. This is what people are supposed to be like. He is the first-born of a new race of human beings. When you see the human Jesus, you see the Father's exact reflection not just because of his divine personality but also because of his humanness.

When we say that there is a humanness in God, we are saying that we see that the perfect man, the good man, is the image of his Father. And the greatest thing is that it is the plan of the Father and of Jesus that we should be remade, recast into that same image. "For whom he did foreknow, he also did predestinate to be conformed to the image of his Son, that he might be the firstborn among many brethren." (Ro 8:29) That is why we can call Jesus "Our Brother"; he is the firstborn, our big brother. In the Southern part of the United States it was the custom for many generations to refer to the oldest child simply as "Brother" or "Sister". Those around always knew what this meant. If there were four boys and three girls of a certain couple, when someone said "ask brother" or "get sister" it always meant ask the firstborn or go get the firstborn. This firstborn was always responsible to help the parents in a special way, to be the example and a care giver and a protector. The Christian can always "ask Brother". Now God wants lots of other children who are like "Brother".

There Is No Reason For You To Be Ashamed

"For, is it not a thing clear as noonday, that if you are ashamed to think the holy soul of Jesus should inhabit mortal and corruptible flesh, which must first be a little purified before the Divine glory will consent to tabernacle in it, then you will be also ashamed, after you have been sanctified of the Holy Ghost, to confess the sinfulness of your own flesh." [10]

Many Christians try to tell themselves that their flesh is not as bad as the Bible says it is. They do this because they do not know of any way out of the dilemma. They want to do the right thing and they want to please God. Actually, we are much happier when we do please God. But, like Paul expressed in Romans 7, we fail to do this. There is a way out. Paul and John both knew about it as well as the other disciples. (Ro. 8: 1-3 and I John 3:20 -21) Contrary to what some teach there is not instant purification in the way we live. We try and continue to fail. The right answer is always the best answer. The right answer is to admit that we can not do it and discover the secret of success in God. What you are reading in this book will enable you to do just that. Once you are established in this you will not have to be concerned about being contaminated by contact with others. Jesus did not worry about this and he was susceptible to temptation and weakness. You have been provided for. Here you are learning how.

What This Can Do For You

---

[10] Edward Irving, *The Doctrine of the Incarnation Opened,* 127.

But we should not stop here. By living in the flesh he conquered the flesh and made it a friend again of God. We can not only afford to be human; God wants us to be human. God's love is contained in human love now in Christians. For a long time Christians have acted like their loving was something imposed upon them by God because "in my flesh dwells no good thing".(Rom. 7:18) There is old flesh and there is new flesh. Jesus lived in flesh to give us new flesh. At the resurrection there will be a new body, even Martha believed this (Jn.11:24). But now, in life, there are new emotions, new truth and a new will to serve God. If it is hard, if it is a teeth grinding effort, something is wrong. It hasn't really happened for you yet. You may be a believer but you are still trying to do it the hard way. You didn't know. His body is food indeed. You are, after all, what you eat. If you eat a lot of sugar, it becomes a part of you. If you eat a lot of cholesterol, it becomes a part of you, clogs up your blood vessels. If you eat healthy food, your body is healthy. If you eat of Jesus, you become like him. Self-improvement is in style these days. Jesus has a better way. The will is most important. Your mind and your emotions follow your will. Jesus had some trouble with his will. At the last he said, "Not my will but yours be done."(Lk. 22:42) He gives us a new will. He causes us to will and to do what pleases him. (Ph.2:13) Paul tells us this just after he tells us that Jesus emptied himself to become a man. We do not have to presume that God's will must always be unpleasant to us. If it is, we are not changing. We do not have to always presume that what we want is wrong. If it is sin, it is wrong. But if we are changing, we will want what he wants.

People often want answers from God. And they can not hear because somewhere back in their mind they have become convinced that God's will must be unpleasant and hard. If you hear something pleasing, then it can not be an answer from God. It is only hard if you are not changing. I delayed giving my life to God because I was afraid I would have to go to Africa if I did. Finally, someone told me that I would not have to go to Africa. Many years after I became a Christian and a minister, I started to want to go to Africa. I finally went and I loved it. I love Africa. It is beautiful and it is fun. I have seen more there working with missionaries than any tourist will ever see. I have been many times and it is always wonderful. The zebra, the giraffe, the antelope, the elephant, sunset on the Serengeti, the sight of Mount Kilimanjaro in the distance, the friendliness of the people of different tribes, the birds in so many colors, the sunlight itself, getting sunburned on a mountain when you feel cold, heat waves around a water hole, wow!

We can be changed. It is no wonder that people do not want to become Christians when they watch Christians who are always straining under the yoke of their faith. Jesus said that his yoke is easy, his burden is light. (Mt. 11:30) Why? Because he came to live perfectly in the flesh so that we can also live in his new flesh. It's all right to be human. God wants it that way. If we have seen him, we have seen the Father. Because he came and we have the gospels, we have the Holy Spirit. We can see. We also have each other. Communion and community are both important. We partake of the flesh of Jesus and we fellowship with the members of his body. If we believe in his plan, we can see him there too. Sometimes maybe not quite in focus, but there all the same.

His Perfect Faith

One man saw it this way. "We hold that [Christ's human nature] received a Holy-Ghost life, a regenerate life, in the conception: in kind the same which we receive in regeneration, but in measure greater, because of His perfect faith: which perfect faith he was enabled to give by being a Divine Person, one of substance with the Father." [11]

What is perfect faith, after all, except the ability to believe totally. Jesus encourages us all through the Gospels to believe and not to doubt.

---

[11] Edward Irving, *The Orthodox and Catholic Doctrine Of Our Lord's Human Nature*, vii.

Doubt is the absence of faith; fear is the destroyer of faith. Jesus' human nature was just like ours. He had to resist sin. Temptation was real to him. Weakness was real to him. But he had perfect faith because of his Divine nature which is just like the Father's. He did better than we do, he did everything perfectly. He fulfilled the law. He still had that link with us in his humanity. His humanity was not even like Adam's before the fall. It was just like ours, only he was born-again at the moment of conception and never needed to improve. Some may say that it was unfair for him to tell us to have faith because he had a Divine nature that gave him perfect faith. But neither Jesus or the Father are ever unfair; what they require, they provide a way to perform. What they say, they do. We can grow in faith more and more. The new birth, and the Holy Spirit enable us to do this. We do not have perfect faith but we do have the opportunity to work towards that goal. It is a real possibility for us to have faith that is 80 percent or even 90 percent perfect. And when we need a boost, there is always grace.

The Holy Spirit

"The Holy Ghost sanctifying and empowering the manhood of Christ even from His mother's womb, is the manifestation both of the Father and of the Son in His manhood . . .so that in the manhood of Christ was exhibited all of the Godhead that shall ever be exhibited, Father, Son and Spirit; according as it is written, 'In Him dwelt all the fulness of the Godhead bodily,' or in a body."[12]

Just as the Holy Spirit did it for Jesus, he will do it for you. Your sameness with Jesus in flesh is the key to your sameness with Jesus in the Holy Spirit. Next, we will want to see how Jesus changed what he got here, what he got back, and what we can have now and later by the Holy Spirit. Then you will need some extra help because your faith is not perfect like Jesus' was, but that is provided for you with what we call Outrageous Grace. You also need to know how to hear God's voice.

The Spirit Of Anti-Christ?

Hereby know ye the Spirit of God: Every spirit that confesseth that Jesus Christ is come in the flesh is of God: And every spirit that confesseth not that Jesus Christ is come in the flesh is not of God: and this is that [spirit] of antichrist, whereof ye have heard that it should come; and even now already is it in the world. 1Jo 4:2-3. AV

Sometimes I read a verse for many years thinking I understand what it means and then, one

---

[12] Edward Irving, *The Doctrine of the Incarnation Opened,* 124.

day, it suddenly becomes clear to me that I did not really understand it until that moment. This is not because I am ignorant of scripture but because scripture has a depth of meaning that we can not comprehend all at once. The Bible is not a book like any other book. It is special.

It is so important to believe that Jesus came in our flesh. There is no other kind of human flesh. The apostle John says that if anyone denies that he came in the flesh then that person is antichrist. This is how John felt about it. Few Christians have ever felt this strongly about it. But John was Jesus' best friend. He was always with him during his ministry. He walked with him and sweated with him. He was tired with him. He talked late into the night with him. John laid his head on Jesus' chest at the last supper. Jesus gave his mother into the keeping of John from the cross instead of to his natural half-brothers, the other sons of Mary by Joseph. And Jesus appeared to John on the Isle of Patmos and gave him the Revelation. John outlived all the other apostles and died when he was past 100 years old. John was the grand old man of the New Testament church. So John knew how important this was. And this is the proper interpretation of the verse. Jesus came in our flesh. He was tempted like we are. He never gave in. He changed that flesh into a flesh that serves God. He took it to the cross and he raised it from the dead.(Jn.10:18) Yes, after death Jesus was restored to full power and raised his body up glorified just like he said he would. This truth will revolutionize your life. Once inside you there will be no reason for you to be ashamed to admit the failings of your flesh ever again.

John says that anyone who does not confess that Jesus Christ has come in the flesh is anti-Christ. It is obvious that John is very serious about this. Does he say that God came in the flesh? Not exactly. Does he say that Christ came in the flesh? Not exactly this either. He says that Jesus Christ came in the flesh. Does this mean merely that the Son made an appearance on earth to be seen by people and accomplished his work? Not exactly. What does John mean when he says that they are anti-Christ? Does this mean that any non-believer is anti-Christ? A heathen, a Buddhist, a Hindu? The best word for them is unbeliever or non-Christian. When John says to try the spirits, he does not mean just ask a demon when he manifests himself. He means to test the truth of any teaching by this concept. Even "friends of Christendom" like the Roman centurion knew that a man named Jesus, who was considered by many to be the Messiah or Christ, walked around in the land of Israel.

This does not just refer to the mere fact that he was here. It refers to the fact that as God, and John makes it plain that he was God in many places, Jesus came in the flesh, in flesh like the flesh of every person. The spirit of anti-Christ is not a spirit or a belief that does not recognize the Christ. This is an unbeliever. The spirit of anti-Christ is one that seems to be Christian but is really against the truth; an insider who is really not inside but a betrayer of the truth. Not one that denies that God was here, but one that denies that he came as a real man. This is anti-Christ and John hates this with a terrible and a holy passion. Who knew the real humanity of Jesus better than John? No one. Did Paul? He never met the unglorified Jesus as far as we know. Did Peter? Even he was not as close as John. Did Mary his mother? Yes, but she left no records. John knew it all. And even in his lifetime some were starting to deny it. That is what he says. Already they are here. They deny that Jesus of Nazareth, the Christ, was really a man in real flesh, body and soul, like we are. This is deception and this is anti-Christ.

If John felt so strongly about this and if it was already at work during his lifetime, what should be our attitude about this? It has had centuries to dig into the church by now. And we should not be passive about this. Granted we do not persecute people about this because we do not "fight against flesh and blood" but against "spiritual wickedness." And we also "strive to convince every man." But we should be convinced, we should speak up. Why is it important? It is important to the life of every believer because Jesus came to be just like we are so that he would be one of us. He knows that he is one of us and we know that he is one of us. He has it all back now, but he went without a lot of it for 33 years. And we have a lot more to get as his inheritors. He came to be one of us so that we could do the same things that he did in the same way that he did them. We can even "do greater things." He did them by faith and he tells us to do them by faith as well. That is how important this is.

David J. Keyser

V. God was in Christ

God was in Christ reconciling the world unto Himself. II Cor 5:19a

How He Changed It

Here it is. This is what will make the difference. This short part of a verse has usually been understood like this. God sent Jesus into the world. Jesus was part man and part God. He did all the right things and said all the right words. Then he went to the cross to take the punishment that sinners deserve so that they could claim his free gift of salvation. This would mean that God would accept the sacrifice of Jesus to pay for their sins. Then God would love the sinner and grant him forgiveness of sins and eternal life. After physical death he will go to heaven to be with Jesus and God the Father.

Much of this is correct. But not all of it. God did send Jesus, but Jesus also agreed to come. Jesus was not part man and part God. He was entirely man and entirely God. This is important because it is not a 50/50 split; he is 100% God and 100% man. He did say all the right words and do all the right things. He did make the sacrifice so that we could claim the gift by faith. But this did not make God love us. God loved us from the start. (John 3:16) We are forgiven and we do have eternal life. However, this life starts now. It starts now in the inner life, the feelings and the thoughts and the will, and even spills over into the body for healthier living. Later we will get a new body that will not grow old or get sick or ever die. But this is still not all.

Jesus said that his body was food indeed and his blood was drink indeed. When he tells us to eat and to remember, he wants us to remember that he has fixed his flesh. His flesh, his thoughts, his feelings, his will are in agreement with God.

For what the law could not do, in that it was weak through the flesh, God sending his own Son in the likeness of sinful flesh, and for sin, condemned sin in the flesh: (Ro 8:3)

You are free to be as human as he was. The thing is, how human was he? He was really human as we have seen in our previous discussions. You live in His flesh. He says to you, "Are you having trouble with your flesh? Here, have some of mine. I have fixed mine. And I did it so that I could give it to you." This is the real meaning of communion with Jesus. You should take communion frequently with an honest heart.

Here is an illustration. When a person has leukemia, which is a blood disease, the doctors often give them a bone marrow transplant to combat the disease. The blood cells are made inside the bones of the body, in the marrow. With leukemia a person has unhealthy blood cells. This will kill them physically if something is not done. God can and does heal people by prayer and the laying on of hands and anointing with oil. But often he uses the doctors. To give a bone marrow transplant they take some healthy marrow from a compatible person with a large needle that they push clear into a bone, into the marrow. They usually use the pelvis for this. Then they put this marrow into the person with the leukemia and a lot of the time the healthy marrow dominates the unhealthy marrow and healthy blood cells are produced. Spiritually, this is what Jesus does when he gives us his flesh. His flesh, which is healthy because he has subdued it, takes over in us. When we partake of his flesh in faith, we receive it by the Holy Spirit. Another thing that is interesting about the bone marrow is this. When they put the marrow into the person who is receiving it, they do not inject it into the bone like they got it out. They just inject it into the flesh and it knows where to go. It goes straight to the marrow and does its work. Now if God can design a physical procedure that works like this, can he not also design a spiritual procedure to get the changed flesh of Jesus into our inner lives?

Jesus' flesh is changed because he changed it. He wrestled it to the ground over a period of 33 years so that he could say at the end, "the prince of this world comes, but he has nothing in me."(Jn

14:30) There was nothing left in his flesh that the devil could use. Jesus had won. Now we can win.

But he got back even more. This was at his resurrection and when he ascended back into heaven. And that is what we will talk about next.

What He Got Back: The Holy Spirit

As the Spirit of God the Father, the Holy Spirit is sent to us as Someone who is really different than we are. When He expresses himself, it is majestic and somehow strange. But we know that it is the Spirit of God and we are thrilled with His operations. The differentness itself is both startling and refreshing. This is how the people of the Old Testament understood God and they were a unique people set apart among the people of the earth.

As the Spirit of Christ the Holy Spirit comes to us and operates within us and through us as One that is familiar. It is good that the church decided after long consideration of the scripture that the Spirit proceeds from both the Father and the Son. The reason that His presence and His gifts and ministries seem familiar to us is because He is the Spirit of Christ who is not only fully God but also fully a man. The Old Testament people of God did not know the Holy Spirit as the Spirit of Christ. In order for this to happen the Son had to become a man and live and minister as a man by the power of the Holy Spirit here among us. When the Holy

Spirit comes to us and works through us as the Spirit of Jesus Christ, He is fully "at home" in us. Therefore, when He suggests something to us or wants to act through our minds and hearts and bodies, He does not do it as a foreigner.

This emphasizes the fact that the humanity of Jesus is also a key factor in the ministry of the Holy Spirit through people under the new covenant. The feelings and actions of the Holy Spirit in and through us are spiritual and also fully human at the same time. They are so friendly that often we do not realize that they come from Him, and as a result we suppress them since we humans are the ones that are in control of their release. "For the spirit of the prophet is subject to the prophet." (I Cor 14:32) For instance, the Holy Spirit, who lives within us as the Spirit of God and the Spirit of Christ, quietly whispers to us something about a person that could not be naturally known. We speak it out as a Word of Knowledge and it is received with wonder and thankfulness and the person who spoke it is praised as a prophet or the like. But we may say, "It was so easy." We need not expect it to come in a trance or other unnatural event. He interfaces with people naturally because He is the Spirit of Christ. There is no strangeness about Him. So when we are not sure if a thought is ours or His, it is because He participates in our thought processes naturally. We should not expect there to be a strangeness in His tone or attitude. He works in cooperation with us.

Only occult experiences which are satanic operate unnaturally in people; this is because evil spirits come uninvited. Evil spirits come to tempt us and they try to sound inconspicuous and they even have a familiarity with human minds and bodies. But their presence is not ever gentle; they have no respect for human kind. The Old Testament talks about "familiar spirits" which specialize in interfacing with the human understanding. They try to imitate the voice of the Spirit of Christ. Sometimes we must ask for discernment to recognize these spirits and we must "test the spirits".(I Jn 4:1) In matters of doctrine evil spirits will not call Jesus Lord or admit that He has come in the flesh. Just because it is possible to be misled by evil spirits, we still can not expect the Spirit of Christ to impress us unnaturally in order for us to take heed because we are the Body of Christ. If an individual is unsure where some knowledge or leading is coming from, the other members of the Body are there to help.

Also, it is important that we learn to function in the Spirit on a continual basis. If we are functioning in a carnal manner, the voice of the Holy Spirit will be difficult or even impossible for us to hear. That is a major part of the entire relationship which is our responsibility, the desire to walk according to the Spirit and not according to the flesh "For the carnal mind is enmity against God." (Rom. 8:7)

Take another example. Often the Spirit of Christ leads believers through what they see or hear externally. Some sight or words may make a particular impression on our minds. We wonder why some simple everyday things seem to be highlighted to us. It is the Spirit of Christ within showing us something. I know a man who went to Africa as an evangelist and people started bringing orphans to him. He looked for a place to get rid of the orphans. Then one day he saw a dump truck with many men in the back. He knew that they were being transported to work because that is how they often transport workers there. But he was impressed that it would be a terrible waste to throw away so many good men. He understood why he had that impression and kept the orphans and became well known as an orphanage founder and director in that African country.

The Spirit of Christ speaks in simple ways. When a person is first filled with the Holy Spirit, every movement of that Spirit within him seems magnified. It is all startling. After a while things quiet down inside. Sometimes, they wonder if they are still filled. Refillings are, of course, good and necessary. Sometimes, they wonder if they have sinned and the Spirit of Christ has deserted them. This too is possible. But many times they do not understand that we are designed by God to host this gentle Spirit. Jesus said that he was "meek and lowly in heart" and that we would "find rest for our souls."(Matt. 11:29) The Spirit of Christ is just like Christ. We must walk with Him in peace. When He empowers us or guides us or speaks through us, it happens easily and naturally.

What We Get Now

First and foremost, we can have the inner nature of Jesus. And this is something that we can grow in. We grow in our awareness of what we have. We grow in allowing the Holy Spirit to put our flesh on the cross of Christ. We grow as we partake of his flesh which is food indeed. We partake at communion and we also partake of the "hidden manna" as we live an overcoming life. But there is more.

The Gifts Of The Holy Spirit

The gifts of the Holy Spirit have been available throughout the Christian era. Some historians will say, "why weren't they more in evidence down through the centuries?" They have been more plentiful during times of the movement of the Holy Spirit. But they have always been available. True, there are times when He moves and times when He does not. There may be many theories as to why this is so. Many would say that prayer is an important factor. When God's people pray, then the Spirit moves. This is generally true. But at other times He surprises everyone when He moves. But this does not change the fact that the gifts have never been withdrawn from the church.

When God's people are taught that they can have the gifts, then someone will no doubt take a step of faith and receive them and begin to walk in them. The question, "How shall they hear without a preacher?" (Rom 10:14) holds true for the gifts of the Holy Spirit as well. Instances where the Spirit is not moving and people are taught to receive His gifts prove that they have never been withdrawn. Edward Irving and his followers in the eighteen hundreds in England and Scotland are a case in point. Here, instead of being surprised by an experience and turning back to the scriptures to see what was happening to them, Irving's followers proceeded on an organized teaching from the Bible and received as they had been taught. And, as is often the case, one strong truth teamed with another intensified their experience. They learned not only about the availability of the gifts but also about the humanity of their Saviour and older Brother. They were taught that the only reason that the gifts had not been exercised over the years was because the faith of the church was so low that they did not expect the gifts. [13] This

---

[13] C. Gordon Strachan, *The Pentecostal Theology of Edward Irving* (Peabody, Mass., Hendrickson, 1973), 15.

condition existed because no one had preached the gifts to them.

"When speaking in tongues did occur in earlier times and among the Huguenots and the Jansenists, it was always one of many phenomena generated by religious enthusiasm and intense evangelical feeling. . . . It has been thought by many from 1830 to the present day that this was also the case in the west of Scotland, at Regent Square, and among the members of the Catholic Apostolic Church. Nothing could be further from the truth. For unlike any previous manifestations of the Spirit, they were occasioned not by the overflow of powerful religious feeling but by faithful response to the systematic study and preaching of the Word of God. Theological understanding was central to all that happened and preceded all forms of experience of spiritual gifts. It is the centrality of a coherent theological system which makes the Pentecost of 1830-32 unique and quite distinct from all previous revivals." [14]

The Holy Spirit only imposes gifts on the church when that is the only way He can give them. It would be much more pleasing to God if His people would "covet earnestly the best gifts." (I Cor. 12:31)

---

[14] C. Gordon Strachan, *The Pentecostal Theology of Edward Irving*, 14.

Divine Miracles Or Works of Faith?

Although the results would be the same either way, there is a difference between a Divine miracle wrought by God Himself and the miraculous result of the faith of a man. If Jesus performed these things as acts of his faith as a man, then we can and should follow him in them. It is important that we understand this for the sake of our present faithfulness and the continuing work of the Body of Christ today.

It is not an insult to attribute an act of faith to the human Jesus. If he loved us enough to limit himself with our limitations and the Father loved us enough to agree, what tribute is it on our part to refuse his gift and just say that he did these things because he was God. The self-limitation of Jesus was an act of love. What he did while subject to these limits was not just to demonstrate to us that such things could be done by a human being, although that in itself is a good lesson, but also to completely share our lot and condition. He has been everywhere we could go. He has taken a flesh like our own to the heights thus making human flesh honorable again. Honorable because without sin he took human flesh through a complete life cycle and even after death raised flesh and bone back to life again. This was not an act of weakness or confusion on his part but an act of love and compassion from the deepest wisdom of God.

If the Bible is true, then it should be taken at face value. Jesus did not perform an act or a pantomime for our benefit. He actually lived it.

VI. How You Function

It is not possible to count the number of times Christians have said, "Well, that was Jesus!" This is said when someone challenges another's faith. "You can do that if Jesus did." "Well, that was Jesus!" The point is exactly that it is Jesus because it is Jesus in you. This is not, of course, what we will call an across-the-board grant. We should especially say that Jesus did not do whatever he wanted to do. Jesus did the will of the Father. You can also do the will of the Father. Let's take an example. The day that Jesus healed the man at the pool Bethesda (John 5) we are told that there was a great multitude of sick people there waiting for the troubling of the waters. But Jesus, so far as we know, only healed one person there. We do not know why he did not heal them all. In another place we are told that he healed all the sick. Perhaps he was just waiting to be asked. Very often we do not have because we do not ask. But we do know that He always did the will of his Father. This we also can do. How? How do we do the will of the Father? We do it in <u>exactly the same way</u> as he did. The Bible says "He that is joined unto the Lord is one spirit. (I Cor 6:17) When we become a Christian, our human spirit merges with the Holy Spirit himself. We will represent this from now on with the word S/spirit. We listen to our S/spirit and act accordingly. You might ask, "If this is true why doesn't every Christian do it? Why don't the Christians that I know do it? Why don't they do miraculous things? Why don't I? There are several obstacles which get in our way.

For one thing we do not know the secret of the S/spirit. We do not know this because we have not been taught it. And behind that we do not understand the humanity of Jesus so we can not identify with him as we should. For another thing we do not understand about the giftings given to Christ and the church. We think to have a gifting means that we can do anything at any time. Jesus had every gifting but he did only what the Father told him to do. We are to do like he did.

If we understand the humanity of Jesus, we will know several things. We will know that he did not act independently but only as the Father told him. We will know that the things that he knew and the things that he did he knew and did by the power of the Holy Spirit which was in him as a man and not because he was and is God. This is sometimes hard to grasp but it is very important. Jesus did not have an "edge" on you because he was God. He functioned by the same Holy Spirit that you do. He came to show us how to function as his larger body. Now, he did have an edge on you because he was without sin. But he has provided a way for you to recover from this which we call Outrageous Grace. Jesus also had to be without sin in order to be Savior. He is the only one who can be Savior. But we can act in his place.

So, after we understand how he was just like us, operating by the leading and power of the same Holy Spirit, we also understand that even if we are not yet sinless, not yet fully grown spiritually, we can still operate like Jesus because he and the Father knew all this long before we came along and they made provision that we should not have to live under a cloud of guilt and ineffectiveness just because we are still "in process". If God had to wait until we were really ready, he could never use anyone and the work of the church, the body of Christ, would never get done.

Then, all that is left is to learn about your S/spirit. You are like Jesus; he was like you. The "wall" of guilt is removed. You no longer have to hide from God. But in order to function as Jesus did, you must know how to hear your S/spirit. The Holy Spirit will train your mind to be able to listen. Start by asking questions of your S/spirit. You can do this at any time because he is always with you. Ask questions that can be answered simply, with a "yes" or a "no". Often the answer is not a verbal one; it is just an impression. Start asking about things that are not important. That way you will not be anxious about the answers. Anxiety will cause a lot of inner "noise" and make you unable to understand the answers. A "yes" might just be a nod, as when a parent is training a child. All the child has to do is look at the parent or listen for her and the slightest sound or look or gesture will communicate the needed guidance or, sometimes discipline. After you can understand yes and no, you can go on to other things. On days when you are having a hard time hearing, you can go back to the yes and no method. As you learn to hear the unimportant things, you can then learn to know more important things because your confidence will be strong.

Your S/spirit is a wonderful guide because it is really a part of you and it is really God also. Since God's Spirit is so big, he will dominate. Therefore your S/spirit will not be wrong. You can understand it in a wrong way with your mind because your mind is still growing, but your S/spirit will not be wrong.

What We Get Later

What we get later is based on what Jesus has now. He is the first person of a brand new race of people, a super race. Not a super race like any of the twisted claims of the past. This race will be composed of people from every country and race in the world. These people will have eternal bodies. There will be no sin. There will be no sickness. No one will grow old. These bodies will have flesh and bone just as Jesus' does. (Luke

24:39) We will live on a new earth and walk also in a new heaven.

Things That Help

The True Humanity Of Jesus Christ, Outrageous Grace and the Three-Part Nature of Human Beings have all been lost or partially lost for generations. In this time of Holy Spirit renewal and restoration they are much needed treasures that need to be returned to the church. We have been considering the True Humanity of Jesus so far in this book. Now on to the subject of Outrageous Grace.

Our Biggest Problem Is Solved

The second secret is what I call "outrageous grace." Now this is really nothing more than the plain old grace that Paul talks about in the New Testament. But it is necessary to call it "outrageous grace" because most believers think of it as a doctrinal position. Many can even define it as "the unmerited favor of God" but it does not have an effect on their daily lives. They do not understand how unmerited it is, or how much favor there is, or how God really feels about it all. This too may be somewhat of a stretch at first but it is well worth the effort to really get a hold of it. For one thing it goes a long way toward putting you, as a believer, on a near-equal footing with the human Jesus as a person can get.

How They Are Related To Each Other

Outrageous Grace, Supernatural Manifestations, and the Glorious Return have usually been symptoms of heightened religious fervor. They are very much bound together and have usually been so bound. The Humanity of our Lord has not been so common. It was a hallmark of the Irvingite movement in the late 1820's and early 1830's. That movement, as has already been discussed, was, however, unique in that it came into existence not as a divine surprise but as the result of the systematic teaching of Edward Irving. And, even though he felt defeated by the events that followed, he never yielded his conviction that he had taught the right thing. The renewed interest in Irving as the "father of 20th century Pentecostal and charismatic movements" shows that there is also a significance to his teaching. The modern movements were not born of teaching. They had to construct their teachings as they went along, hopefully at the leading of the Holy Spirit but sometimes, regretfully so, not at His leading.

What is needed today in the church at large is a thorough understanding of these concepts which are all born of God. The Reformation began to get a hold on grace and faith, but this has only survived in a very narrow portion of the church at large. It needs to be brought back with zeal; grace, outrageous and glorious, and the faith which only it can inspire.

Interest in a Supernatural God is born out of a move of the Holy Spirit. But millions today are interested in any thing which exhibits the supernatural. Many are searching blindly and in ignorance and if the church will again present a supernatural God, it will draw people to God and to His people no matter what name they gather under.

An expectancy of the Glorious Return will often flow from an awareness of the presence of the Holy Spirit. It was true for Tertullian and the Montanists; it was true for Irving and his followers; it has been true for the Pentecostals and the charismatics; and it will be true again. One thing will amplify another again and again. Like an audio feedback loop.

Most of us at one time or another have been in a room where a microphone squeals horribly. What is happening there is an audio feedback loop. The microphone is set at too sensitive a setting so that it takes any noise that it hears and amplifies it until it hears it again and then amplifies it again and so on and so on. By the time we hear that horrible squeal it has looped around hundreds of times to produce what we are hearing. These understandings about the things of God will amplify each other. The heat will increase like logs together in a fire.

The teaching of the humanity of our Lord Jesus Christ will add much fuel to the spiritual fire. Now is the time. His humanity will speak to hearts. His divinity will not be sacrificed. We need to be willing to think the unthinkable. Jesus is strong; he will not break. Never will we give up our belief in his divinity or his total lack of sin. But we have not realized yet exactly how much he became like us. Therefore, we will always say things like, "Well, He was Jesus. He was God. I have to live 'down here' after all." Such sayings reveal that we cannot identify with him. If we understand the other concepts, they can not burn as bright without this understanding of His humanity. I believe that we absolutely can not understand the others without at least beginning to understand His humanity as he lived it almost 2,000 years ago and as it exists today.

However, we will not be able to "think the unthinkable" without some grasp on Outrageous Grace. Do you kill your children for testing limits? You may discipline them; so does God. But what if they never tested limits? Would they ever grow up to be functioning adults on their own? Does God want his children to always take the 'safe road'. All you have to do is look at King David and Moses and Abraham and Peter and Augustine to see that it is the heart that matters to God. Push grace in everything. God is big enough to rein you in. Especially push grace in regard to considering the humanity of our Lord.

Push Grace

What does it mean to "push grace?" Sometimes, we think that the grace of God is fragile. We think that if we disappoint him too often, he will give up on us. The better we get to know God, the more we realize that this is not true. You see, God has an attitude. We often talk about a person having "an attitude". But almost always this is a bad attitude that we are talking about. God does not have bad attitudes. His attitude is this: if He loved you before you even knew about him, before you cared anything about him, then He is not going to stop loving you no matter how many times you let him down.

"But God commendeth his love toward us, in that, while we were yet sinners, Christ died for us. Much more then, being now justified by his blood, we shall be saved from wrath through him. For if, when we were enemies, we were reconciled to God by the death of his Son, much more, being reconciled, we shall be saved by his life." (Ro. 5: 8-10)

God's attitude is that now we are children instead of strangers. He will always take us back and help us. But more than this, God wants you to take chances with Grace and Faith. Now some may say that this is presumption; and it can be. We do not want to be presumptuous. But more often than not we are too careful. We do not believe that God will back us in a pinch. How many earthly fathers will back a child in front of people even if he punishes him later. We need to push grace. We need to expect more. Sometimes, it is the only way to escape the bondage of legalism. God is big enough to keep us in check. We have no foundation of righteousness to offer God. If your heart is set on him, you will improve. If every time you stumble you resolve to try harder next time, you are doomed to failure. You have to count on the Holy Spirit to change you and cause you to improve and to grow. You need to agree, but he needs something to agree with. Agree with the Holy Spirit. Push grace.

"Sin, therefore, is a pre-requisite of grace; and only a sinner can be the subject of grace: others may know goodness, but sinners alone can know grace. Grace is not goodness, nor is it harmony, nor is it wisdom, nor any other attribute of God which is exhibited in creation; but it is that power and liberty which remaineth in God after all these have done their work, and seen that work frustrated by sin, to come in a second time, and out of the ruins build a more glorious temple that the first, so framed and fashioned as to reveal hidden treasures of the Godhead which the first could never bring to light." [15]

That is what grace is. You have to be a sinner to use grace. Grace is a power of God and a liberty of God Himself. He builds better things out of ruins that anyone else can build with new materials. As a matter of fact, he builds so good with ruins that what you see after he is done is better than what was there in the first place. How about that? What a wonderful thing the Grace of God is. That is why I call it Outrageous Grace. If anyone but God invented grace or used grace, it would have to be wrong. But God did it. And it is right and good. And even better, we can use it too, for ourselves and towards others. Go ahead and forgive him, it will do him good. Go ahead and accept her back, it will do her good. And you too!

There is a part of you that knows. It is important to understand that every believer is composed of three parts even before they become a Christian. These parts are body, soul and spirit. (I Thess. 5.23) Many have been taught that the words "soul" and "spirit" are merely two different ways of saying the same thing. This is not true and it is stupid when you really stop to think about it. Why would the Bible, which those who hold that soul and spirit are the same thing and will fight to protect the accuracy of the Bible, use two words

---

[15] Edward Irving, *The Doctrine Of The Incarnation Opened,* 1828, 313-314.

for the same thing unnecessarily? No, they are indeed very different parts, both internal and invisible, but very definitely not the same thing. Those who hold that they are the same, effectively rule out or cancel entirely, the whole function of the human spirit. The human spirit is not the Holy Spirit. It is that created part of us which is most like God for "God is a Spirit" (John 4.24). And because it is most like God, it can communicate with God and understand Him better than the soul. Of course, the soul is important and it is with the soul that we think and feel and make decisions. But the spirit can hear from God after a person becomes a believer and the Holy Spirit moves in and is joined with the human spirit forever.

These Three Work Together

It is important to know that these three wonderful secrets work together in the life of the believer to make her or him wonderfully effective as a Christian. You can not separate them from each other. If you do not understand the True Humanity of Jesus, you can not identify with Him as you need to. If you leave out Outrageous Grace, you will be crippled in your spiritual walk. If you do not know the difference between your soul and your spirit, you can not hear from God. In this little book we have explored all three of these wonderful secrets. After you learn them and study them, your Christian walk will never be the same again.

You will need to know the difference between your S/spirit and your mind. There are several guidelines for this. Ultimately, you will just learn by experience because God is a good teacher. And you always have him with you. But some guidelines can help.

First and foremost, your S/spirit will not try to tear you down in any way. Isn't that wonderful? Your mind might try to discourage you. Often it does. This is because your mind is opened to suggestions from the sensory world around you, from other people and from the devil. But your S/spirit is totally renewed and is joined to the Holy Spirit. Because God is a God of grace your S/spirit will always hear the Grace Message. Even if God is correcting you, the grace message will still be there to provide the "way of escape" and the forgiveness and restoration that you need. You are responsible to repent. God will always forgive. And your S/spirit will constantly hear this message. This message is always consistent with the written Word of God. This Word has the effect of dividing your soul from your S/spirit so that the Grace Message can predominate in your life. When the Word divides your soul from your S/spirit, it is sometimes through conviction and sometimes through comfort and sometimes it is through both. Sometimes, you do not even know how it happened because you were not reading the Word on a subject that you understood to be related to your current problem or blockage in your spiritual walk. But you were reading the Word and it did its job just like it says that it will. (Heb. 4:12) Then you not only hear the Grace Message from your S/spirit but you can hear any leading that God has for you as well. "As many as are led by the Spirit of God are the sons of God." (Rom. 8:14)

www.ingramcontent.com/pod-product-compliance
Lightning Source LLC
LaVergne TN
LVHW011411080426
835511LV00005B/484